P9-CDW-036

LIVE
WITHOUT
FEAR

LIVE WITHOUT FEAR

Learn to Walk in God's Power and Peace

DR CREFLO A. DOLLAR

New York Boston Nashville

Unless otherwise indicated, all Scripture quotations are taken from the *King James Version* of the Bible.

The author has emphasized some words in italicized type within the Scripture quotations. These words are not emphasized in the original Bible versions.

FaithWords Edition
Copyright © 2000, 2004 by Dr. Creflo A. Dollar
Creflo Dollar Ministries
2500 Burdette Road
College Park, GA 30349

All rights reserved. Except as permitted under the U.S. Copyright Act of 1976, no part of this publication may be reproduced, distributed, or transmitted in any form or by any means, or stored in a database or retrieval system, without the prior written permission of the publisher.

Revised in 2006

FaithWords
Hachette Book Group
237 Park Avenue
New York, NY 10017

Visit our Web site at www.faithwords.com.

Printed in the United States of America

FaithWords is a division of Hachette Book Group, Inc.
The FaithWords name and logo are trademarks of Hachette Book Group, Inc.

First Hachette Book Group Edition: March 2006
10 9 8 7 6 5 4 3

LCCN: 2005937853
ISBN: 978-0-446-69843-6

Contents

Introduction

Fear is a very serious attack that the enemy uses against the human race. It is imperative to learn how to defend ourselves against this evil. Fear intends to destroy our faith and harvest. Fear comes in many shapes and sizes, but the final outcome is the same—to steal, kill, and destroy.

Fear has gripped our generation like never before through terrorism. Believers cannot be moved by this attack. God has provided the ability to overcome fear at every turn and know that faith brings us the victory. It is God who fights our battles. When we are confident in that, fear cannot besiege us.

Before I published this book in 1994, the Lord spoke to my heart and said, "Teach people how to drive out fear from their lives. Don't just address the surface issues, but teach them to dig up the root." That prompted me to do an intensive search of the Scriptures for what God has to say about fear and how to be free of it.

When I think about God's people living in terror, in spite

of the fact that they are in a literal kingdom of priests (Rev. 1:6) who wield the very authority of Heaven itself, I get angry. Fear has no place in the life of a believer. God's Word gives us clear, practical principles that, if diligently applied, will banish fear from our lives forever.

It's time to declare war on fear.

LIVE
WITHOUT
FEAR

This Thing Called Fear

F EAR, SIMPLY DEFINED, is "a dread, uneasiness, or anxiousness." But from a biblical standpoint, *fear* is more than a feeling, it is a spirit.

Second Timothy 1:7 says:

> God hath not given us the spirit of fear; but of power, and of love, and of a sound mind.

When a believer is influenced by the Holy Spirit, we call it an *anointing*. This anointing of the Holy Spirit empowers and emboldens ("gives courage to," or "causes to be bold"). His empowerment enables a Christian to do things they could never do in their own strength and wisdom.

In a sense, the presence of a spirit of fear in your life also brings with it an "anointing"—a negative, destructive anointing.

- Instead of empowering you, fear paralyzes you.

- Instead of giving you wisdom, fear causes you to make poor decisions.

- Instead of the blessing of the true anointing of the Holy Spirit, the demonic anointing of a spirit of fear brings a curse.

You may be thinking, "Pastor Dollar, do you really expect me to believe there is such a thing as a demonic anointing?"

Yes, child of God, I do expect you to believe that, because it is biblical. Test all things by the Word of God.

Look at Mark chapter 5 where we are told about the "madman of Gadara." Possessed by a legion of demons, this man was able to break chains and perform other superhuman feats. He was able to do this through the "empowerment" of the demons, or through a demonic anointing of supernatural power.

This satanic "anointing" also turned him into one of the most miserable, wretched creatures you can imagine. That is always the outcome of demonic "anointing." The "anointing" that comes with a spirit of fear will make you miserable and wretched.

Principles Governing Fear

According to Romans 8:1,2, there are two basic spiritual laws in operation in the earth today. One system is dominated by life, and the other system is dominated by death.

There is therefore now no condemnation to them which are in Christ Jesus, who walk not after the flesh, but after the Spirit. For the law of the Spirit of life in Christ Jesus hath made me free from the law of sin and death.

In those two verses, we can see the two basic domains under which Christians can and must operate:

1. One is called the "law of the Spirit of life in Christ Jesus."

2. The other is called the "law of sin and death."

Every human being today is living his life under one or the other of these two "laws." All human beings ever born have lived under one of these two laws. There are no other choices. The sad part is that even being born again does not mean a Christian lives his life under the right law.

A *law* is an established principle that can be expected to function the same way every time. For example, the "law of gravity" applies to everyone in every situation and every place. A rock dropped from the top of a building will fall the same every time.

The same is true of the two spiritual laws. If you are living under the "law of sin and death," there is no way to avoid receiving sin-oriented and death-oriented results. Just like the falling rocks, this principle brings the same results for everyone who lives under it.

These two spiritual laws are very different from one another, but they are more than just different. They are "reciprocals," as 2/3 is the reciprocal of 3/2. Both are fractions, yet one is the upside-down version of the other. They are opposites.

The "law of sin and death" is the upside-down opposite of the "law of life in Christ Jesus."

For every spiritual force and substance in the realm of life, there is a reciprocal force or substance in the realm of death.

- In the first, you will find the force of hope.

- In the other, you will find its reciprocal—despair.

- Under the "law of life," you will find *agape* love, the kind of love that gives and gives.

- Under the "law of death," you will find the reciprocal of *agape*—total selfishness.

One of the most powerful forces in the realm of the law of life in Christ Jesus is the force of faith. According to God's

Word, faith can move mountains and work miracles. The universe itself is the product of faith-filled words. (Heb. 11:3.)

Faith's Reciprocal

Faith has a reciprocal under the "law of sin and death." As you may have guessed already, it is called fear.

In fact, fear always rushes in when faith is not present. We get a clear picture of this very thing happening in one of the incidents in the ministry of Jesus. This is the familiar story of Jesus sleeping in a boat while the disciples were awake, weathering a storm on the Sea of Galilee.

> *And his disciples came to him, and awoke him, saying, Lord, save us: we perish.*
>
> *And he saith unto them, Why are ye fearful, O ye of little faith? Then he arose, and rebuked the winds and the sea; and there was a great calm.*
>
> Matthew 8:25,26

Do you see the connection Jesus made?

"Why are you *afraid?* You have little faith."

He was attributing their fearfulness to a lack of faith. Mark and Luke related the same story in slightly different words.

And he said unto them, Why are ye so fearful? how is it that ye have no faith?

Mark 4:40

And he said unto them, Where is your faith? And they being afraid wondered, saying one to another, What manner of man is this! for he commandeth even the winds and water, and they obey him.

Luke 8:25

In all three reports, we can see Jesus declaring the reciprocal relationship between fear and faith. He could not declare it any plainer than this:

If you have faith, you will not have fear.

If you have fear, it is because you have little faith.

This reciprocal relationship goes much deeper even than you might think. Perhaps you know that attention to God's Word brings faith onto the scene:

So then faith cometh by hearing, and hearing by the word of God.

Romans 10:17

But did you realize that attention to Satan's words brings faith's reciprocal, *fear*, into your circumstances?

For example, if you pay attention when the devil whispers into your ear that you are going to go broke, fear will soon grip your soul. Before long, you will be walking around wringing your hands and losing sleep, fearing that you are going to go bankrupt and lose everything.

Naturally, that kind of fear then opens the door for the devil to enter and begin really playing havoc with your finances. Soon your worst fears have been realized.

"I knew it all along," you will wail. "I knew this was going to happen!"

Fear gives place to the devil, thus allowing him to operate freely. That was precisely what took place with the disciples in the storm-tossed boat. Their fear in the beginning stages of the storm gave Satan room to really start tearing things up.

Fear allowed the storm to get to a point where it might have destroyed them. That is why Jesus exclaimed, "Where is your faith?" when He woke up.

In essence, He was saying, "Why is this happening? Why is there water in this boat? Why have you allowed your fear to generate this circumstance rather than taking authority over it by faith?"

There is no way for Satan to operate destructively in your life unless you give place to him.

You may ask, "How do you 'give place' to the devil?"

You give the devil place by paying attention to his words and thereby beginning to operate in fear.

If you were to receive a bad report from a doctor saying that you only have three months to live, the enemy is immediately going to be in your face, saying, "It's true! It's true! You've had it! You are going to die."

However, if you know what the Word of God says about Jesus, ". . . by whose stripes ye were healed" (1 Pet. 2:24); and, if you know what God said about those who set their love on Him, "With long life will I satisfy him . . ." (Ps. 91:16), then you will not listen to the enemy.

If you pay attention to the devil's words and the doctor's report rather than the Word of God, fear will immediately begin to wrap its icy fingers around your heart. Unchecked and unreversed, fear will open the door for the devil to come in and kill, steal, and destroy. All the praying and wailing in the world will not make a bit of difference, because your fear has given place to the devil to do his destructive work.

Fear comes by hearing, and hearing means "by words." (Rom. 10:17.) Fear may come through the devil's words whispered directly to your mind, or it may enter through the words of other people. For example, fear may enter through your paying attention not only to a doctor but to a friend or relative speaking negatively. Even the words of a newscast declaring that the economy is failing or that it is not safe to drive the streets at night can make a way for fear to enter.

Any message of doubt can bring fear. Guard the "gates" of your soul. Your eyes and ears are gateways to your mind and spirit. If you allow the unceasing torrent of disaster, calamity, and tragedy that flows out over the airwaves to enter your gates day in and day out, it will not be long before you are afraid to leave your home, much less do the things God has called you to do.

No matter where it comes from, if it does not line up with God's Word, what you hear and pay attention to is an open invitation to the destructive spirit of fear.

Declare War on Fear!

God hath not given us the spirit of fear; but of power, and of love, and of a sound mind.

2 Timothy 1:7

My prayer in the power of the Word . . .

_____

_____

_____

_____

_____

_____

_____

Study Questions

1. What do you most fear in this world?

_____

_____

_____

_____

_____

2. What would you say is the source of your fear?

_____

_____

_____

_____

3. What does the Bible say conquers fear?

_____

_____

_____

_____

4. How does faith drive out fear?

_____

_____

_____

_____

_____

2

Hire the Right Team

We have seen that two reciprocal laws operate in the spiritual realm where human beings are concerned: the "law of the Spirit of life in Christ Jesus" and the "law of sin and death."

We have also seen that two reciprocal forces energize each of these laws. On the one hand, faith energizes and activates the law of life. On the other hand, fear (faith's reciprocal) activates the law of death.

Each of these pairs represents a team, and no matter who you are, one of these teams is working for you right now.

What determines which team is on your side? *Your choices,* particularly your choice of words, determine which team is on your side.

How do I know that? Look at Proverbs 18:21:

*Death and life are in the power of the tongue: and they
that love it shall eat the fruit thereof.*

Death and life: The two laws about which we have been talking are in the power of the tongue, the Bible says. In other words, what you say can activate either the one law or the other.

You "employ" one or the other of these teams through your words. Either you hire the fear-and-death team, or you hire the life-and-faith team. Once hired, they go to work to bring about the only fruit they can.

Here is how this works:

When symptoms of sickness attack your body, you will be tempted to tell everyone how badly you feel. "Oh, I'm sick. I'm probably going to be in bed for days. I'm afraid I may lose my job."

If you give in to that temptation to feel sorry for yourself and get sympathy from others, you will be hiring the fear-and-death team. The only fruit that team can produce is destruction, loss, and pain.

On the other hand, if you resist that temptation and declare, "By the stripes of Jesus I was healed 2,000 years ago; therefore, I am healed," you will be hiring the life-and-faith team. This team goes to work immediately to carry out what God's Word has decreed.

By speaking what God's Word says about your situation,

you activate the law of life in Christ Jesus. Faith then comes through the hearing of the Word of God. However, you should remember that a team can be fired as quickly as they were hired.

If you get impatient waiting for the manifestation of your healing and say, "This isn't working; I really am sick," and so forth, then you have just fired your faith team. Once you employ the team of life and faith on your behalf, do not fire them by speaking things contrary to what the Bible says about your circumstances. Apply the force of patience. *The Word works!*

Team Reinforcements

Although the reciprocal forces of faith and fear are very powerful in and of themselves, the two teams we have been discussing have other members as well. One of the most powerful of which are angels, heavenly and fallen.

There are demonic forces, and there are heavenly forces.

Heavenly angels hearken to the Word of God. When you employ the life-and-faith team through speaking the Word of God, you marshall armies of angels who go into action to bring about what the Word has declared.

By the same token, fallen angels or demons respond only to the words of Satan. When you repeat the words the devil has whispered in your ear—words such as, "I'm going to fail," "I'm going to go broke," "I'm going to die," or "My husband is going to leave me,"—demons go into action because they now have a license to bring to pass the very thing you have spoken.

Both types of angels are enforcers of the law under which they operate:

- Heavenly angels enforce the law of life.

- Demons are the enforcers of the law of sin and death.

Would you like an army of angels working on your behalf to enforce God's covenant promises found in His Word?

Then begin to speak faith-filled words. Find out what has been written in the Bible about your situation and say that. Do not fire this amazing team by giving place to fear or doubt. Turn a deaf ear to the devil's lying whispers and never, never speak them out.

We will talk more about angels and how to put them to work for you in the last chapter.

The Establishing Witness

You probably are aware of the biblical principles that state: "by two or more witnesses a thing is established" (Deut. 19:15; Matt. 18:16; 2 Cor. 13:1; 1 Tim. 5:19; Heb. 10:28). In other words, from Heaven's perspective, it takes at least two parties saying the same thing for a matter to be settled.

For example, when God's Word says, ". . . by whose [Jesus']

stripes ye were healed" (1 Pet. 2:24), but the devil says, "You're going to get cancer and die," you have two different parties saying opposite things.

Obviously, one is true and one is false. However, concerning your situation and your life, those opposite statements make a one-to-one tie, and you are the witness who establishes one or the other in *your* life. Whichever position you come into agreement with through your will, words, and actions will be binding in your life. You choose whether truth will prevail, or whether getting in agreement with a falsehood will allow the devil to bring destruction into your life.

Many believers blame God, a minister, or other people for results that actually are direct results of their own words and actions. As a child of God, if you go broke, it is probably because you sided with the devil and his lying words through your speech rather than agreeing with God's Word that says:

> *My God shall supply all your need according to his riches in glory by Christ Jesus.*

> Philippians 4:19

To break free of fear and the law of sin and death, you must stop mindlessly validating whatever your physical senses perceive. What you see, hear, and feel is transitory. It is subject to change. The Word of God is true, unchanging, and eternal. If what you feel is contradictory to the Bible, choose to endorse with the fruit of your lips what the Word of God says.

You are the establishing witness. Whichever law you validate with your words and actions will be the law under which you live.

However, if you have established the wrong law in your life, take heart. There is a way out. God's mercy has made a way for us to turn things around when we take the wrong road.

Declare War on Fear!

My God shall supply all your need according to his riches in glory by Christ Jesus.

Philippians 4:19

My prayer in the power of the Word . . .

_____

_____

_____

_____

_____

_____

_____

Study Questions

1. What role does teamwork play in the life of a Christian?

_____

_____

_____

_____

_____

2. What successful teams have you been on?

_____

_____

_____

_____

3. How can a believer begin to team with the angels to enforce the law of life?

_____

_____

_____

_____

_____

4. What would you say to someone who argued, "But I can't *see* angels"?

_____

_____

_____

_____

_____

3

Breaking the Bondage of Fear

*F*EAR BRINGS BONDAGE.

There is no getting around that fact. When a spirit of fear takes root in your life, you become a slave to that fear. This fact is really a principle that is stated clearly in Hebrews 2:14,15.

> *Forasmuch then as the children are partakers of flesh and blood, he [Jesus] also himself likewise took part of the same; that through death he might destroy him that had the power of death, that is, the devil;*
>
> *And deliver them who **through fear of death** were all their lifetime **subject to bondage.***

A fear of death or of any other aspect of the law of sin and death brings with it an awful bondage. The good news is that

Jesus paid the price for our freedom. Those two verses in Hebrews tell us that one of His purposes in allowing Himself to be crucified was to "deliver them who through fear" have spent their lives in bondage to fear.

Whatever type of bondage a person is involved in—cigarettes, drugs, sex, food, or anything else—fear produced it.

I have had people tell me, "I'd quit smoking, but I'm *afraid* I'll gain weight." Fear! Bondage!

If fear invariably produces bondage, what does fear's reciprocal—faith—produce? Faith produces liberty, of course!

Faith brings freedom, which is why the devil works so hard to keep Christians in fear and out of faith. If he cannot take a person to hell, he will at least try to keep that person bound up, paralyzed, and ineffective as a Christian witness. If any Christian ever gets hold of faith and the liberty faith brings, the devil knows he is in trouble!

For a believer in Christ Jesus to live in bondage to fear is as unnatural as a fish trying to live out of water. Part of being born again is being born to freedom, being released from bondage to sin. And fear is sin, because the Bible says that whatever is not of faith is sin. (Rom. 14:23.) The Apostle Paul wrote:

> *For ye have not received the spirit of bondage again to fear; but ye have received the Spirit of adoption, whereby we cry, Abba, Father.*

> Romans 8:15

Fear is totally alien to your reborn spirit. In fact, your spirit cannot produce fear. It has to come from the outside. You can receive fear, but you cannot manufacture it. You can act on it. You can be choked by it and let it paralyze you. *Only* you, by an act of your will, can keep this from happening. This truth is echoed by Paul in 2 Timothy 1:7:

> *For God hath not given us the spirit of fear; but of power, and of love, and of a sound mind.*

Fear is never from God. I have heard religious people talk about God giving them a "healthy fear" of something or other. Child of God, there is no such thing as a "healthy fear." If it is fear, it did not come from your Heavenly Father. The verses quoted in this chapter prove that.

Fear Requires Repentance

You may want to stop reading at this point and repent for the fears in your life. Ask God to cleanse you through the Holy Spirit of all lack of trust in Him. If a spirit of fear has taken strong control of your emotions to the point where you are driven and motivated by fear instead of faith in God's Word, then you may need to go to your pastor for prayer and counseling.

In the rest of this book, you will learn how to uproot fear from your mind and how to stay free of fear. I want you to see what you have as a Christian:

25

As a Christian, you are an heir of salvation. (Heb. 1:14.)

As a Christian, you also are an heir of protection. You are wrapped up, tied up, and tangled up in the righteousness of God. You have nothing to fear.

It will help you to look through the Bible for all the occasions in which Jesus or an angel said, "Fear not," to some person. God knows that nothing of spiritual value can be accomplished in your life until you get rid of fear. Over and over in Scripture, God commands His servants not to be afraid.

Why should we not fear?

A Christian should never fear, because Jesus said, "I will never leave thee, nor forsake thee" (Heb. 13:5).

It is an insult to God to allow circumstances to cause you to fear when the all-powerful Creator of the universe has sworn to stand by you.

Fear is sin because it means not trusting your heavenly Father and not believing His Word. Fear has a companion that sticks very closely to it, aiding and abetting fear's ability to get hold of you. You will hardly ever find fear without this companion. We will take a look at this in the next chapter.

Declare War on Fear!

For ye have not received the spirit of bondage again to fear; but ye have received the Spirit of adoption, whereby we cry, Abba, Father.

Romans 8:15

My prayer in the power of the Word . . .

_____

_____

_____

_____

_____

_____

_____

Study Questions

1. In what ways does fear bring bondage?

_____

_____

_____

_____

_____

2. In what ways does fear bring freedom?

_____

_____

_____

_____

_____

3. Why does fear require repentance?

_____

_____

_____

_____

_____

4. What steps could you take right now to begin conquering fear?

_____

_____

_____

_____

_____

Doubt Is Fear's Companion

FEAR'S FAVORITE "SIDEKICK" is *doubt*, sometimes translated "unbelief" in the *King James Version* of the Holy Bible.

Actually, *doubt* is fear's "advance man." An advance man is one who goes on ahead of someone, some group, or some ministry to prepare the proper reception for the ones he represents. Doubt almost always makes an appearance in your thinking before fear comes along. Doubt's job is to prepare you to receive Mr. Fear when he arrives.

One of the best biblical examples of how doubt runs interference and results in fear can be found in Matthew 14:25–31. This is the account of Jesus walking on the water.

> *And in the fourth watch of the night Jesus went unto them, walking on the sea.*

And when the disciples saw him walking on the sea, they were troubled, saying, It is a spirit; and they cried out for fear.

The disciples panicked, thinking they were seeing a ghost.

But straightway Jesus spake unto them, saying, Be of good cheer; it is I; be not afraid.

We all too often need to hear this as well as the disciples.

And Peter answered him and said, Lord, if it be thou, bid me come unto thee on the water.

And he said, Come. And when Peter was come down out of the ship, he walked on the water, to go to Jesus.

But when he saw the wind boisterous, he was afraid; and beginning to sink, he cried, saying, Lord, save me.

And immediately Jesus stretched forth his hand, and caught him, and said unto him, **O thou of little faith,** *wherefore didst thou doubt?*

In those verses, Jesus clearly attributed Peter's fear and failure to doubt. Keep in mind that giving attention to the Word of the Lord puts you in the realm of the law of life. As long as Peter was focused on Jesus' word, "Come," he was able to operate in the realm of the miraculous.

But when Peter shifted his focus to the waves and the wind, removing his focus from Jesus and the Word He had spoken, he stepped out of the law of life and entered the domain of sin and death.

What was the result? Peter got wet and began to fear that he was going to drown.

What caused this shift in Peter's focus? According to Jesus, doubt shifted Peter's focus from faith to natural circumstances.

Doubt pulled up alongside Peter and said, "Take a look at the size of those waves!"

Then Peter, choosing to operate by his senses rather than the Word, paid attention to doubt and looked at the waves.

Then doubt whispered, "You're a pretty good swimmer, but if you were to sink in wind and waves like these, you surely would drown!"

At this point, the advance man, doubt, had done his job. Peter was primed and ready for fear to make its appearance. Peter was no longer focused on Jesus and the Word He had spoken. He had moved from faith to doubt and from doubt to fear. All that was left for him to do was yell, "Help!"

In a like manner, many believers get hold of a little bit of the Word and begin to learn how to walk on top of the waves of their circumstances. As long as they focus on Jesus, the Word of God, and the covenant they have with the Lord through the new birth, they walk in victory.

What they do not realize is that the devil will use the same strategy on them that he used on Peter. A demon will try to get them into doubt so that fear can have an invitation to enter. Peter fired faith and re-hired fear, and so do many Christians.

Satan's strategy was actually initiated in the Garden of Eden. This trick was successful in getting Adam and Eve to betray God.

The Origin of Doubt and Fear

Adam and Eve had a Word from God telling them they could eat of all the trees in the Garden except one. Eating of the tree of the knowledge of good and evil would be absolute disobedience to God's Word and rebellion against the Most High. This act brought death into the world, which God had warned them would be the case. (Gen. 2:16,17.)

The way Satan approached Eve was to cast doubt on God's Word.

He said, "Did God *really* say this? Yes, but what was God's motive? Why won't He let you eat of this wonderful tree?" (Gen. 3:1.)

Adam and Eve listened to Satan and then acted on the doubt and disbelief in God that had been seeded into their minds. Once they moved into doubt, they were easy prey for sin. As always, the end result was death and bondage to fear.

And the LORD *God called unto Adam, and said unto him, Where art thou?*

And he said, I heard thy voice in the garden, and I was afraid, because I was naked; and I hid myself.

Genesis 3:9,10

The devil wants you to doubt God's promises.

The devil wants you to doubt God's faithfulness.

The devil wants you to doubt the power of the Word and the power in Jesus' name.

He knows that when you are in doubt, the door is wide open for fear. When you are into fear, you have moved right back under the domain of the law of sin and death. Then you have problems.

Perhaps you have made that journey from doubt to fear. If so, you probably are sinking right now.

You may be sinking in debt.

You may be sinking in sickness.

You may be sinking in marital or family problems.

Whatever the case, I have good news for you. Jesus is as merciful and patient today as He was in Peter's day.

Cry out, "Lord! Save me." Then purpose to get your focus back on Jesus and the Bible. Choose to operate only in the law of life in Christ Jesus.

Say, "I'll no longer be moved by what I hear, see, or feel. I'll no longer be subject to the laws that govern the natural world. I choose not to be governed by the law of sin and death. I'm free!"

If cancer comes calling, and a doctor tells you that you only have three weeks to live, say, "No! I'm not going to operate in that law. I am going to operate above cancer."

The key in maintaining that position of faith is to resist doubt. If the devil cannot get you to doubt God's promises and His Word, fear does not stand a chance. As long as Peter was focused on Jesus telling him to come to Him, then he strode above his circumstances.

When you get a Word from God, hold on to it like a pit bull and never turn loose. Symptoms and circumstances may be screaming for attention. Doubt may be shouting in your ear. But, no matter what is going on, stay on the Word.

If your stormy sea is financial, get a word like, "God will supply all my needs according to His riches in glory." (Phil. 4:19.)

If you find yourself in a hurricane of sickness, latch onto "I am the LORD that healeth thee" (Ex. 15:26), and do not let go.

Resist doubt. Resist it with all your being. If you can remain standing on the Word of God, the victory is yours. Remember that you have "Christ in you, the hope of glory" (Col. 1:27), not the hope of disaster.

Do not walk in fear.

Do not walk in doubt and open yourself up to fear and disaster.

Making the Decision

You must decide once and for all to uproot the destructive spirit of fear from your life. Doing that requires a quality decision. Why the urgency? If everything we have seen in the world up to this point is not reason enough for driving fear from your heart, simply do it because God said for us to "fear not."

He said this over and over in Scripture. Take Isaiah 43:5, for example:

> *Fear not: for I am with thee: I will bring thy seed from the east, and gather thee from the west.*

Or how about Isaiah 41:10:

> *Fear thou not; for I am with thee: be not dismayed; for I am thy God: I will strengthen thee; yea, I will help thee; yea, I will uphold thee with the right hand of my righteousness.*

All of these statements are "covenant statements." When you understand the strength of your covenant with God and get a revelation of His covenant faithfulness, you will not be afraid, even in the most overwhelming of situations.

What do you think gave David his confidence when he faced Goliath? Look at what he shouted at the giant:

> . . . For who is this uncircumcised Philistine, that he should defy the armies of the living God?

> 1 Samuel 17:26

Circumcision was the sign of the Abrahamic covenant with God.

David was saying, "I have a covenant with Almighty God, and this guy does not. I don't care how big he is, he does not stand a chance against me."

That is precisely the attitude God wants you to have. To attain this type of confidence, you must recognize that you too have a covenant with God (a better one with better promises, according to Hebrews 8:6).

David's covenant was backed up by the blood of bulls and goats. Your covenant is backed by the very blood of Jesus Himself. Also, you have His mighty name backing you up—a name at which every knee must bow. (Phil. 2:10.) You have all the authority and power of the Father, Son, and Holy Spirit backing you up.

Furthermore, as a believer, you have the right to dwell in "the secret place of the Most High."

> *He that dwelleth in the secret place of the most High shall abide under the shadow of the Almighty.*
> *I will say of the LORD, He is my refuge and my fortress: my God; in him will I trust.*

Psalm 91:1,2

Declare War on Fear!

Fear thou not; for I am with thee; be not dismayed; for I am thy God: I will strengthen thee; yea, I will help thee; yea, I will uphold thee with the right hand of my righteousness.

Isaiah 41:10

My prayer in the power of the Word . . .

_____

_____

_____

_____

_____

_____

_____

Study Questions

1. How would you define *doubt*?

_____

_____

_____

_____

_____

2. Where does doubt come from?

_____

_____

_____

_____

_____

3. Why does doubt erode our spiritual lives?

_____

_____

_____

_____

_____

4. What counsel would you give to a Christian friend who was experiencing doubt?

_____

_____

_____

_____

_____

5

"What I Have Greatly Feared . . ."

THERE IS ANOTHER compelling reason for driving the spirit of fear from your life. This reason is the unchanging spiritual principle that *fear becomes a magnet to attract the thing you dread the most.*

This principle goes all the way back to Job:

> *For the thing which I greatly feared is come upon me,*
> *and that which I was afraid of is come unto me.*

Job 3:25

Contrary to popular religious belief, the terrible things which happened to Job did not unexpectedly strike because the devil got permission from God to bring those things to pass. Job had been living for years in fear and dread of those things happening. In fact, one of the first things we are told about Job is that he was "continually" offering sacrifices for his children. He was afraid they might have committed some awful sin.

> *And it was so, when the days of their [his sons] feasting were gone about, that Job sent and sanctified them, and rose up early in the morning, and offered burnt offerings according to the number of them all: for Job said, It may be that my sons have sinned, and cursed God in their hearts. Thus did Job continually.*

> Job 1:5

Job was consumed with fear:

- He was afraid his children were going to curse God.

- He was afraid he was going to lose everything as a result.

As we discover in subsequent verses, Job's fear caused God's hedge of protection around him to be lifted. God did not lift the hedge; Job's fear did. His fear became a magnet that attracted the very thing he dreaded the most.

> *For the thing which I greatly feared is come upon me, and that which I was afraid of is come unto me.*

> Job 3:25

It is not hard to see how this could be once you understand the two laws we discussed in the opening chapters. As you have seen, faith and the peaceful confidence which it brings activates the law of life in Christ Jesus. Under this law, there is no disaster, no calamity, and no harm.

Fear, on the other hand, activates the law of sin and death. When Job allowed a stronghold of fear to take root in his life, he was wide open to whatever the devil wanted to do to him, and God was honor-bound to let it happen! Why? This happened because it was Job's choice to live in fear rather than faith in the promises of God.

God Respects Our Choices

God will never override your will. He will respect your choices. Now, I know that no person in his or her right mind would ever choose to be sick, poor, or stricken by tragedy. However, we do often choose to give heed to the devil's words rather than God's Words. And, as we have seen, fear is the reciprocal of faith. It works the same way, only in the negative.

Just as the force of faith goes to work to bring about the good things God has promised, fear—when activated—goes to work to bring about the very thing of which you are afraid. How does fear come? Remember what I wrote in an earlier chapter? Fear comes by hearing, and hearing by words of the devil.

In fact, any principle in the Bible which involves faith and its ability to bring good things to your life, will also apply to fear and its power to bring destruction to your life. For example, we are told in Romans 10:10:

> For with the heart man believeth unto righteousness;
> and with the mouth confession is made unto salvation.

Just as heart-belief and mouth-confession of God's Word brings about the blessings of salvation, when you have fear in your heart and speak it out loud with your mouth, it brings about destruction. That is why fear is a magnet for the things of which you are afraid. When you operate in fear, the law of sin and death goes into motion to bring about the very object of your fear.

As a pastor, I have seen this principle in operation many times:

- A woman lives for years in fear of getting cancer. Her mother had it. Her grandmother had it. She reads about it and studies up on it. She talks about it, and one day, she gets a grim report from her doctor: She has developed cancer.

  "I knew this was going to happen," she cries.

In Job's words, she is saying, "The thing I greatly feared has come upon me."

For the thing which I greatly feared is come upon me,
and that which I was afraid of is come unto me.

Job 3:25

• Another man is consumed with a fear of getting
robbed. He walks down the street eyeing with suspicion
everyone he meets. He is ever careful, constantly on
guard. In the spirit realm, this man has a flashing red
neon sign over his head saying, "Rob me!"

One day he will pass a person with a history of robbery,
and the man fearful of robbery will become a victim of
a robber. It is practically inevitable. Like the law of
gravity, the law of sin and death works every time for
everyone. There are no exceptions.

"But, Pastor Dollar," you may say. "Won't telling people
this make them even more afraid?"

I am not writing this to scare anyone. I am writing about
these principles because they are truth and to motivate Christians to take steps to eliminate doubt and fear from their lives.
I want to see my brothers and sisters in the Lord living under
the blessings of the law of life in Christ Jesus.

Examine yourself. What are you afraid of? What worries
and anxieties consistently occupy your thoughts?

Are you afraid you will never find a suitable wife or husband?

Are you afraid of losing your spouse?

Are you afraid that your children are going to rebel and be harmed?

Are your fears health-related, financial, or relational?

Identify your fears, then attack them.

Make a quality decision right now to uproot that fear which has plagued you for years. Purpose to remove it. Do not wait for it to manifest before you take action. Do it now!

Declare War on Fear!

For with the heart man believeth unto righteousness; and with the mouth confession is made unto salvation.

Romans 10:10

My prayer in the power of the Word . . .

_____

_____

_____

_____

_____

_____

Study Questions

1. In what ways does fear attract the things we dread most?

_____

_____

_____

_____

_____

2. What are you afraid of?

_____

_____

_____

_____

3. What worries occupy your mind?

_____

_____

_____

_____

4. Take a moment to write down your fears, bring them before the Lord in prayer, and tell the Lord you intend to conquer them.

_____

_____

_____

_____

_____

Fear of Man

Up to this point, the types of fear we have examined have been related primarily to circumstances, such as sickness, tragedy, and financial hardship. There is, however, another type of fear that is just as common and equally destructive. It is the *fear of man*. Far too many Christians are living lives of bondage to fear of people.

I am talking about not doing or being all that God has called you to do and be because of the influence of another person or because of their opinion. The Bible is filled with examples of this kind of fear in operation.

The adult generation of the men of Israel who came out of Egypt failed to enter the Promised Land because of fear of man, which amounted to *intimidation*.

The Israelites came to the very edge of the promised land,

the land of which God had said, "I give you this land. Go take it, and I will be with you. I will give you the victory."

In preparation for the invasion, they sent out twelve spies to check out the enemy. One of the twelve, Caleb, was full of faith and confidence in the Word of the Lord.

> And Caleb stilled the people before Moses, and said, Let us go up at once, and possess it; for we are well able to overcome it.
>
> Numbers 13:30

Caleb was not simply optimistic. He was enthusiastically confident.

His report to Moses and the people was, "Let's go do it now!"

One of the other twelve, Joshua, agreed with him. The other ten, however, brought back a different report.

> But the men that went up with him said, We be not able to go up against the people; for they are stronger than we.
>
> Numbers 13:31

These ten men chose to believe what their senses told them about the enemy rather than what God's Word said about themselves and about the enemy. As a result, they moved from doubt to fear—fear of people. That fear spread like wildfire through the camp of Israel.

> *And they brought up an evil report of the land which they had searched unto the children of Israel, saying, The land, through which we have gone to search it, is a land that eateth up the inhabitants thereof; and all the people that we saw in it are men of a great stature.*
>
> *And there we saw the giants, the sons of Anak, which come of the giants: and we were in our own sight as grasshoppers, and so we were in their sight.*
>
> *And all the congregation lifted up their voice, and cried; and the people wept that night.*
>
> Numbers 13:32–14:1

Fear is like a cancer. It spreads. Fear of people begins like any other fear—by considering the circumstances rather than the promises of God.

The ten spies saw giants.

Caleb and Joshua saw the covenant Israel had with Almighty God. The same God later delivered David from Goliath, Shadrach, Meshech, and Abednego from the fiery furnace, and Daniel from the jaws of the lions. Compared to the size of Caleb's God, those giants looked like ants.

The spies operated in strong fear; Caleb operated in strong faith.

For us, Canaan is a type of the abundant, victorious Christian life. The passage through the Jordan River is a type of the baptism of the Holy Spirit. When you allow yourself to be intimidated by the outward appearance or manner of other people, you can rob yourself of the glorious inheritance that is yours as a child of God.

Instead of living in the abundance and security of the Promised Land, you live in the scarcity of the wilderness on the other side of the Jordan.

Fear of Disapproval

Have you ever failed to do something you knew God wanted you to do simply because you were afraid of what someone else would think about you?

Have you ever changed your plans because you feared how someone might respond?

Most of us have done these things at one time or another. When we do, we have fallen victim to another form of "fear of people."

We can see a classic example of this type of fear in operation in the life of King Saul, Israel's first king, in 1 Samuel 15. Saul was a man who battled insecurity. The Bible tells us that, although Saul stood head and shoulders above all the men of Israel, he was "little" in his own sight. (1 Sam. 15:17.)

That basic insecurity and the need to please other people led Saul into a "heap of trouble." When doubt and fear developed into a fear of people, it cost him and his descendants a kingdom.

In this account, Saul had been commanded by the Lord through Samuel to go and completely destroy the evil Amalekites. His detailed instructions were to destroy every living thing.

> *Now go and smite Amalek, and utterly destroy all that they have, and spare them not; but slay both man and woman, infant and suckling, ox and sheep, camel and ass.*
>
> 1 Samuel 15:3

That may sound harsh to you, but you must realize that this was an extremely wicked people whose sin was polluting the land and all those around them. Did Saul obey the instructions of the Lord? Read on.

> *And Saul smote the Amalekites from Havilah until thou comest to Shur, that is over against Egypt.*
> *And he took Agag the king of the Amalekites alive, and utterly destroyed all the people with the edge of the sword.*

> *But Saul and the people spared Agag, and . . . the lambs, and all that was good, and would not utterly destroy them: but every thing that was vile and refuse, that they destroyed utterly.*

1 Samuel 15:7–9

Child of God, partial obedience is no obedience at all. A halfway, half-hearted, go-through-the-motions type of obedience is no better than outright rebellion. In fact, it is actually worse.

Jesus said, "I would thou wert cold or hot," not "lukewarm" (Rev. 3:15–16).

Partial obedience is actually disobedience.

Saul's failure to trust God and obey Him came as a great disappointment to both Samuel and the Lord.

Then came the word of the Lord unto Samuel, saying,

> *It repenteth me that I have set up Saul to be king: for he is turned back from following me, and hath not performed my commandments. And it grieved Samuel; and he cried unto the Lord all night.*

1 Samuel 15:10,11

Disobedience always hurts those who love us and are counting on us. In Saul's case, he compounded his sin by trying to cover his disobedience with a lie.

> *And Samuel came to Saul: and Saul said unto him, Blessed be thou of the LORD: I have performed the commandment of the LORD.*
>
> 1 Samuel 15:13

In other words, Saul walked up to God's prophet with a big smile on his face and announced in his most religious tone, "Yea, and verily, brother. I have obeyed the Lord!"

However, Samuel did not buy that. With a strong note of sarcasm in his voice, he asked:

> *. . . What meaneth then this bleating of the sheep in mine ears, and the lowing of the oxen which I hear?*
>
> *And Saul said, **They** have brought them from the Amaletkites: for **the people** spared the best of the sheep and of the oxen, to sacrifce unto the LORD thy God; and the rest we have utterly destroyed.*
>
> 1 Samuel 15:14,15

When confronted with his disobedience, instead of confessing and repenting, Saul became self-righteous *and* he blamed "the people." He claimed that the best of the animals were spared for a sacrifice to the Lord. But Samuel informed him in no uncertain terms that God is more interested in obedience than in some smelly sacrifice.

> And Samuel said, Hath the Lord as great delight in burnt offerings and sacrifices, as in obeying the voice of the Lord? Behold, to obey is better than sacrifice, and to hearken than the fat of rams.
> For rebellion is as the sin of witchcraft, and stubbornness is as iniquity and idolatry. Because thou hast rejected the word of the Lord, he hath also rejected thee from being king.
>
> 1 Samuel 15:22,23

God said, "Rebellion is the same as witchcraft!"

God is serious about His people obeying His instructions. Too many Christians are caught up in religious activity while neglecting the very things God has called them to do. You may be making great sacrifices of time and energy, but it is not pleasing to God unless you are obeying what He has told you to do.

Finally, in 1 Samuel 15:24, we find out the real reason for Saul's disobedience:

And Saul said unto Samuel, I have sinned: for I have transgressed the commandment of the LORD, and thy words: **because I feared the people,** *and obeyed their voice.*

Saul feared the people. His insecurities and need for approval caused him to violate the clear command of the Lord God Almighty. He fell into the trap of thinking that his position came from pleasing people rather than pleasing God. The result of this was that Saul lost everything: his kingship, his anointing, his calling, and finally, his life.

Fear of disapproval is a powerful motivator in the lives of many Christians today. Some will do practically anything to make sure they have the approval and affirmation of their friends, family members, or co-workers.

Approval Is a Hard Taskmaster

Perhaps, like Saul, you have gotten caught up in pleasing other people at the expense of pleasing God. If so, you know it is a form of bondage.

"What other people think" can be a harsh taskmaster.

You can be afraid to look too prosperous.

You can be afraid to look too confident.

You can get so caught up in worrying about the way people perceive you that you become ineffective as a servant of God.

I have liberating news for you: *You cannot please people.*

Someone is going to criticize you no matter what you do. So, you might as well go ahead and please God. Trying to please people will not get your bills paid or your children saved. Pleasing others will not get you healed.

Quit struggling trying to serve other people and get busy serving God! It pays tremendous dividends. The Apostle Paul knew this:

> *For do I now persuade men, or God? or do I seek to please men? for if I yet pleased men, I should not be the servant of Christ.*

Galatians 1:10

As Paul says, you cannot be a man-pleaser and still whole-heartedly serve Christ. The root of all man-pleasing is a spirit of fear; specifically, the fear of people.

Get rid of it, or like Saul, you risk missing out on all the glory and victory God has planned for you.

Declare War on Fear!

For do I now persuade men, or God? or do I seek to please men? for if I yet pleased men, I should not be the servant of Christ.

Galatians 1:10

My prayer in the power of the Word . . .

_____

_____

_____

_____

_____

_____

_____

Study Questions

1. Have you ever known anyone who lived in fear of another? How did it affect their life?

_____

_____

_____

_____

_____

2. Who do you fear? Why?

_____

_____

_____

_____

_____

3. Describe someone who lives with a fear of disapproval. Why does that fear defeat them?

_____

_____

_____

_____

_____

4. Why should a Christian refuse to live with a fear of disapproval?

_____

_____

_____

_____

_____

7

Four Keys to Uprooting the Spirit of Fear

I HOPE YOU are thinking, "Okay, Pastor Dollar! You have convinced me. I want fear out of my life, once and for all."

The biblical principles and concepts we have examined so far will go a long way toward making freedom from fear a reality in your life. By this time, you should also have an insight as to the type of fear you are dealing with personally.

In this chapter, we will break these principles down into practical steps that you can take to uproot the spirit of fear from your heart and mind.

Key Number One:
Make a Quality Decision

To break free of fear, first you must make a quality decision to do this. That may seem obvious; however, it is precisely where many people miss it.

They never come to a point in time where they say, "This is it. I'll not live another day under this yoke of bondage. This ends here and now."

Look at Psalm 118:6:

> The LORD is on my side; I will not fear: what can man
> do unto me?

Did you see what David said in that psalm? *I will not fear!*

He knew that fearing, or not fearing, involved an act of the will. Many believers are sitting around waiting for God's power to strike them like a bolt of lightning so they can be free of fear. Others are waiting for some "mystical" force to rise up inside them. All the time, God is waiting for them to take the first step—the step of choosing.

You got into fear by an act of your will, whether you realize it or not, and you will only get out the same way. Receiving fear and getting rid of fear both require your cooperation and your will.

You choose to accept or reject fear the moment you are attacked by it.

If you are riding on an airplane and the ride gets extremely turbulent, the enemy will come in and whisper, "This plane is going to crash."

The instant that thought comes, you must raise up your shield of faith (Eph. 6:16) and say, "No! I will not fear."

You must, by an act of your sovereign will, choose faith over fear. Then reinforce that by reminding yourself and the enemy of what God's Word says about your protection and safety.

Remember the 91st Psalm and tell the devil you live in the secret place of the Most High. Tell him that a thousand may fall at your right hand and ten thousand at your left hand, but no calamity will befall you. (Ps. 91:7.) God has given His angels charge over you to keep you in all your ways, lest you fall and dash your foot against a stone. (Ps. 91:11,12.) Glory to God! Hallelujah!

Do that, and you will move from the edge of fear into having a faith-filled, "Holy-Ghost fit" right there in the aisle of the plane.

Fear does not have the right to usurp authority over a human being who has made the decision to live above fear. Once you have made the decision to live with fear no longer, it cannot reenter your life without an act of your will authorizing it to do so.

How do you authorize fear? You give it authority in your life by listening to and pondering on devilish words of doubt and unbelief, as we saw in chapter four.

One evening not long ago, I was reading my Bible while another member of my family watched television. All of a sudden, what the newscaster was saying about a rash of drive-by shootings registered in my mind. Alarms went off in my spirit.

I jumped up, grabbed the remote control, and turned off the television newscast.

"I can't listen to that fear-and-unbelief talk," I told my family. "I'm guarding my ear gate against fear."

I have begun to condition myself to immediately shut out words or images that the devil might use to attempt to produce fear in me. I have chosen to rid my life of fear, and I have chosen to stay free. It is important for you to understand that freedom begins with an act of your will.

Look again at the verse we have been talking about, Psalm 118:6:

> The LORD is on my side; I will not fear: what can man
> do to me?

Notice what prompted David to declare his choice not to fear: It was a revelation that *the Lord was on his side*. That same revelation can also make you bold.

Try to remember a situation to which you responded with fear. Now ask yourself a question: If you truly believed God was on your side, would you have handled that situation the way you did? Would you have gotten into fear? No way! When you believe God is on your side, you are calm, confident, and relaxed.

Perhaps you are one of those who wonder if God really is on your side. If you are in covenant with Him through the blood of Jesus, then the answer is a resounding yes! As Paul said in Romans 8:31,32:

If God be for us, who can be against us?

He that spared not his own Son, but delivered him up for us all, how shall he not with him also freely give us all things?

Your heavenly Father is on your side, child of God. Start acting like it.

Key Number Two: Understand the Magnitude of God's Protection

Two of the most exciting verses on protection in all of Scripture are found in Isaiah 43:1,2:

But now thus saith the LORD that created thee, O Jacob, and he that formed thee, O Israel, Fear not: for I have redeemed thee, I have called thee by thy name; thou art mine.

When thou passest through the waters, I will be with thee; and through the rivers, they shall not overflow thee: when thou walkest through the fire, thou shalt not be burned; neither shall the flame kindle upon thee.

Here is truly good news. Not only does God's protection extend to keeping you from being consumed by disaster, violence, sickness, or financial collapse, it will keep you from being affected by any of those things in the slightest way. When you walk through a fiery trial, not only will you not be burned, you will not even come out smelling like smoke.

Notice what this verse does not say: It does not say you will not go through the fire. Some Christians have come to believe they should never have to face a trial or a problem. They are in for a big surprise! Trials and troubles are going to come as long as we are in this world. Jesus told us to expect them. (John 16:33.)

No, Jesus never promised that we would not have problems. However, He did promise that we could be victorious over them because He has already overcome the world.

I do not know what kind of "fire" you may be going through right now, but God said you could walk through it without even being singed.

You can walk through crises without even any signs of worry.

You can walk through trouble with no extra gray hairs, no ulcers, and no headaches.

You can walk through a tidal wave of difficult times and come out dry as a bone.

Notice what else the passage in Isaiah tells us. In it, God said, "I have called thee by thy name; thou art mine." Imagine that! God has laid claim to you.

Suppose you went outside and found someone bothering your child.

In a flash, you would be there, saying, "No, sir! This is my child. To get to her (or him), you will have to come through me!"

When the reality that God feels that way about you sinks down into your spirit and becomes a part of your understanding, fear will have a very hard time getting a foothold in your life again. Knowing this will make you bold.

God has claimed you for His own possession, which means that He has taken personal responsibility for your care and protection. You will stay in that protection unless you choose to walk out from under it of your own free will.

Key Number Three: Develop Confidence in God's Promises

At this point, however, I want to give you fair warning. The enemy's number-one strategy to keep you locked into a lifestyle of fear is to try and keep you in doubt as to the truth of God's promises. This is still his most reliable weapon.

As we have seen, that is the tactic he used to get Adam and Eve to disobey.

This is the strategy the devil tried on Jesus when he tempted Him after a forty-day wilderness fast.

The devil will try to get you to question the authority and

accuracy of what God has said. Why does he do this? It is because God's promises are your weapons against him. Armed with the promises in the Bible, there is nothing you cannot do or be. That is the main thrust of 2 Peter 1:4:

> *Whereby are given unto us exceeding great and precious promises: that by these ye might be partakers of the divine nature, having escaped the corruption that is in the world through lust.*

See how powerful God's promises are? By them, we become partakers of the divine nature. No wonder the devil's main focus is on getting us to disregard them. It is through them that we tap in to the power and nature of God.

Faith in God's promises moves mountains, heals cancers, gets bills paid, restores marriages, and changes the world. So what will the devil use to try to neutralize this power? He will use fear, the reciprocal of faith. Specifically, fear that God's promises are not true.

This battle primarily takes place between your ears—in your mind. It is the first place doubt or fear are going to show up when you begin to stand on God's Word. If you lose it in your thought life, you have lost the war.

For example, if you are standing on God's promises of provision and prosperity to get your needs met, the first time a bill comes due that you cannot pay, you will stand strong.

You will say, "My God supplies all my needs." (Phil. 4:19.)

But if a week or two goes by, and you still have not been able to pay that bill, the devil is going to sidle up to you and whisper, "Maybe it's not working. Maybe you are not holy enough."

And you may say, "No, sir! I am the righteousness of God in Christ Jesus, and my bill is going to be paid."

But in the back of your mind, perhaps a little doubt has been planted.

If the day the bill is due rolls around, and there is still no sign of God's provision, the devil will turn the pressure up a notch or two.

"What are your friends going to think? You told them all that Jesus was going to pay your bills," the enemy will whisper. "Sure, this 'faith stuff' works for other people, but it doesn't work for you."

At that point, unless you have developed your "faith muscles" and trained your thinking, doubts are going to begin to flood your mind. As we have seen, where doubt is, fear is not far behind. Once you are into fear, you can forget about seeing the miraculous provision of God. You have stepped over into the realm of sin and death.

What was the point of the attack? It was to get your mind to entertain a shadow of a doubt concerning the promises of God. How do you counter that? You can counter doubt in several ways:

- First, you must take every thought captive to the obedience of Jesus Christ. (2 Cor. 10:5.) When the enemy calls into question the truth of God's Word, do what Jesus did. Come right back at him with a Scripture, "It is written, Mr. Devil":

So shall my word be that goeth forth out of my mouth: it shall not return unto me void, but it shall accomplish that which I please, and it shall prosper in the thing whereto I sent it.

Isaiah 55:11

- Secondly, add to your faith the force of patience. Patience means remaining consistently the same. Hebrews 6:12 shows us how these two powerful forces work together.

That ye be not slothful, but followers of them who through faith and patience inherit the promises.

You must take the position which says, "Devil, I believe God's Word, and I am not moved by what I see, hear, or feel. I do not care how long it takes for the truth to manifest, I will not be moved off of my confidence in God's Word."

That is the kind of dogged determination the Apostle Paul wrote about in Galatians 6:9.

And let us not be weary in well doing: for in due season we shall reap, if we faint not.

Never forget, "due season" always comes. If you will not faint, you will see that due season of harvest. Things in the spiritual realm take time on earth to put into place.

God promised Abraham that he would be a father. That did not happen overnight. In fact, it took many years.

God told Noah that rain was coming, but it did not come in a month, a year, or even a century. However, the rain was right on time—God's time. There is a due season for everything, and your due season will come, if you will not faint in your mind through doubt.

Key Number Four: Employ Perfect Love

You will find another remarkable key to uprooting a spirit of fear in 1 John 4:17,18:

Herein is our love made perfect, that we may have boldness in the day of judgment: because as he is, so are we in this world.

> *There is no fear in love; but perfect love casteth out fear: because fear hath torment. He that feareth is not made perfect in love.*

Do you want to be free from fear? Then get into perfect (mature) love. If you have fear, there is something in your life in the area of love that needs to be examined. Now, the word translated *love* in these verses is the Greek word, *agape*. That word always means the "God-kind" of love, the kind of love that gives without expecting anything in return.

How do we show this kind of love to God? In 1 John 5:3, the God-kind of love is spelled out for all Christians to see.

> *For this is the love of God, that we keep his commandments: and his commandments are not grievous.*

> 1 John 5:3

Do you want to be perfected, or mature, in the love of God? The way to do this is simple: Keep His commandments. Jesus told His disciples the same thing. If they truly loved Him, they would keep His commandments, He said. (John 14:15.) The word *keep* in John 14:15 simply means "to do," or "to perform."

We have now seen that the key to casting out fear is to be mature and complete in love, and that love is based on obedience. It is not based on how you feel but on what you do. Obedience is the only standard of measure of your love for God. If you love Him, keep His commandments. Grow mature in that kind of love, and fear will not come within "a country mile" of you.

Why is obedience such a powerful force? Perhaps Jesus said it best in John 15:14.

Ye are my friends, if ye do whatsoever I command you.

Friend is a covenant word. When those in covenant with one another in ancient times called one another "Friend," that meant they were acknowledging responsibilities toward one another.

Jesus was saying, "I will call you Friend and Covenant Partner, if you will obey My commandments."

This explains how "perfect love" (obeying God's commandments) can cast out all fear. Fear cannot enter your heart because your obedience to God firms up your covenant with Jesus.

Obedience energizes your heart with faith.

Obedience causes you to do the very things Satan fears you will do—things such as spending time with God, studying the Word, and learning the Word at church.

If you wake up not feeling well on Sunday morning, and the devil, or your flesh, says, "You better just stay home," then that is the time to get to church at all costs. Go just because the devil does not want you to go.

Do not let anything stop you from going to church. Why is that so important? God's Word says not to forsake the assembling together of ourselves. (Heb. 10:25.)

I have learned over the years to be the most aggressive in my obedience in the areas where my flesh and the devil are most reluctant.

For example, there was a time when I had fear and reluctance in certain kinds of giving. Sometimes the Lord would prompt me to give a gift that, in the natural, was quite a stretch for my budget. Before I got hold of these principles about fear, sometimes fear would paralyze me, and I have missed blessings by not giving.

One day, the Lord spoke to me saying, "You are going to have to get rid of that fear."

He helped me do this by setting up a "test," so I would have an opportunity to attack fear.

One night while praying, the Lord said, "I want you to give so-and-so $1,000."

"Lord, that can't be your voice I'm hearing," I protested. "$1,000!"

But it was the Lord. Choosing the path of obedience, I swallowed hard and wrote the check. The power of fear in my life over finances and giving was broken that night. I have gotten increasingly bold in my giving since then. Now I give in faith, not fear. I give knowing that, because I am obedient in giving, it will be given back to me "good measure, pressed down, and shaken together, and running over" (Luke 6:38).

What broke that stronghold of fear? Love broke it, the kind of love for God that shows itself through obedience to His commands. Walking in the love of obedience will get rid of fear for you just the same as it did for me. This works not only in the realm of finances, but in every area of your life—health, relationships, work, or ministry.

Whatever commandment of God the devil is trying to convince you *not* to do, get aggressive in obeying that one. That is the area that is holding you back in spiritual growth.

Declare War on Fear!

If God be for us, who can be against us?
He that spared not his own Son, but delivered him up for us all, how shall he not with him also freely give us all things?

Romans 8:31, 32

My prayer in the power of the Word . . .

_____

_____

_____

_____

_____

_____

Study Questions

1. What quality decision do you need to make to uproot fear in your life?

_____

_____

_____

_____

2. Why is God's protection of His children important in uprooting fear?

_____

_____

_____

_____

3. If a friend came to you asking for help in developing confidence in God's promises, what would you tell him or her?

_____

_____

_____

_____

4. What does the Bible mean when it says, "There is no fear in love; but perfect love casteth out fear"?

_____

_____

_____

_____

8

Three Keys to Staying Free of Fear

THE FOCUS OF this book is to teach you how to uproot fear from your life. It is vital that you know how to do this, because all of us have deep-rooted fears that need to be dug out in order to walk in victory and receive God's blessings. Just as importantly, we need to know how to stay free from fear and how to keep new fears from developing in our hearts, minds, and spirits.

The following keys will help you do just that.

Key Number One:
Live Right

Living right does not change God; it changes you. When you are walking in God's righteousness, doing what you are supposed to do, talking as you are supposed to talk, and acting as you are supposed to act, you have confidence and boldness.

Beloved, if our heart condemn us not, then have we confidence toward God.

1 John 3:21

A man or woman who is living right does not have to fear. When you have confidence before God, it is much easier to stay in faith. As we have seen, faith is the only way to function in the law of life in Christ Jesus.

Key Number Two: Speak the Word

When doubt or fear come knocking at your door, it is vital that you avoid speaking the devil's words. We have seen how dangerous that can be. But simply keeping your mouth closed is not enough. You must generate faith by speaking God's words instead, regardless of the way circumstances look around you.

When the rumor going around the place where you work is that people are going to be laid off, do not join the crowd in wringing your hands and crying, "Oh, Lord, what are we going to do?"

Make it your first impulse to jump up and say, "I'll not lose my job, praise God! I'm a tither and a giver, therefore, I'm blessed going in and blessed going out. Everything I put my hand to prospers."

When the newscasts say that children are being shot,

abused, and abducted at an alarming rate, make your confession this:

"All my children shall be taught of the Lord and great shall be the peace of my children. No weapon formed against them shall prosper!"

Do not do these things one time and then forget it. Confess what God's Word says about your situation over and over again. Do it when you wake up. Do it while you are driving. Confess it to your spouse and friends.

Why is this so important? It is important because, as we have seen, faith comes by hearing the Word of God. Nothing has more impact on your spirit than to hear with your own ears your own voice proclaiming God's Word.

When you are speaking God's promises, the traffic in your mind has to be quiet. The devil has to hush. Your own soul has to hush. The speaking of the Word takes priority.

I remember an occasion before my father had given his life to Christ. I had been praying for him and witnessing to him for some time. One day, I got a phone call.

The voice on the other end of the line said, "Your father has been rushed to the hospital. He has had a heart attack."

Immediately a wave of panic tried to roll over me. I felt fear begin to try to wrap itself around my spirit.

A voice inside my head said, "Your father is going to die without Jesus and go to hell."

Then, realizing what was happening, I got a grip on my

emotions and said, "No! It is not his time to go yet. I have prayed and claimed my father for Jesus Christ. I have promises in God's Word that say I can have what I say when I ask in faith. I will settle down right now and stand on God's eternal Word. In the name of Jesus, my father will not die. He will recover."

Fear left as suddenly as it had come. I went to the hospital, walked into my father's room, and calmly said hello to him.

He said, "How are you?"

I said, "Fine."

Finally, after a long silence, Dad said, "I've decided to get saved."

In a crisis situation, it is vital that you recognize instantly that fear is your worst enemy and begin to quote the Word of God.

Key Number Three: Stay in the Light of the Presence of God

Fear will cause you to try to hide yourself from the light of God. Remember Adam's response after he disobeyed God?

> *And they heard the voice of the LORD God walking in the garden in the cool of the day: and Adam and his wife hid themselves from the presence of the LORD God amongst the trees of the garden.*

And the LORD God called unto Adam, and said unto him, Where art thou?

And he said, I heard thy voice in the garden, and I was afraid, because I was naked; and I hid myself.

Genesis 3:8–10

When you sin, your natural, fleshly reaction is to get into fear and shun the presence of the Lord. The devil will begin to "beat up" on you about how unworthy you are to talk to the Lord or to worship in His house. He will tell you that God is mad at you. The next thing you know, like Adam and Eve, you are hiding out from God in fear, and the devil is having a field day in your life.

Do not fall into that trap. When you miss it—repent! First John 1:9 says:

If we confess our sins, he is faithful and just to forgive us our sins, and to cleanse us from all unrighteousness.

When you make a mistake, move right into the light of God's presence and get it set right. Do not let fear and condemnation make things much, much worse.

As you have discovered from reading this far, a fully developed, oppressive spirit of fear does not appear in you overnight. Usually, it grows over time like a parasitic vine that slowly chokes the life out of a formerly healthy plant.

For a root of fear to begin to grow in you, it must have soil. That soil is your mind.

What are the seeds of fear? They are thoughts. Fearful thoughts enter your mind and, given the right conditions, take root, spread, and grow.

In the next chapter, we are going to look at some ways to deal with these kinds of thoughts.

Declare War on Fear!

Beloved, if our heart condemn us not, then have we confidence toward God.

1 John 3:21

My prayer in the power of the Word . . .

_____

_____

_____

_____

_____

_____

_____

Study Questions

1. As you look at your own life, what changes would you
need to make in order to "live right"?

_____

_____

_____

_____

_____

2. What does it mean to "speak the Word"?

_____

_____

_____

_____

3. How can a Christian stay in the light of the presence of
God?

_____

_____

_____

_____

4. What is God calling you to do or to change today?

_____

_____

_____

_____

_____

Dealing with Thoughts

THE PRIMARY WAY seeds of fear enter your mind is through one of the "gates" of your senses. Seeds of fear can enter through what you see, hear, feel, or even smell. For example, if you are in a crowded building and you smell smoke, what is your first thought?

The devil uses these seeds that enter through the sense gates to make suggestions. In fact, suggestion is one of his most potent weapons. His tactic is to suggest certain words, certain scenarios, certain possible outcomes, all with the intent of planting a seed of fear. All of this takes place in the form of thoughts.

You may be thinking, "How in the world am I supposed to control my thoughts? I have tried, and those fear thoughts just keep coming back."

Do not worry. The first thing you need to realize is that

negative thoughts *are* going to come. It is inevitable. The solution is that you do not have to keep those thoughts.

I once heard a man of God tell a story about a lady who came down to the altar for prayer one Sunday at his church. She was very distraught and upset.

When the man of God asked what was wrong, she blurted out, "I want you to pray for me that I won't have any more bad thoughts."

He smiled at her and said, "Sister, if I could pray that for you, I would pray it for myself!"

He went on to say, "Evil thoughts are going to come. You cannot keep birds from flying over your head, but you can keep them from building a nest in your hair."

His point was that instead of wasting spiritual energy in a futile attempt to avoid bad thoughts, we should refocus our minds on how to deal with those thoughts when they come. You can take or refuse any thought, good or bad. What do I mean by "taking" a thought?

Jesus told His disciples, ". . . Why *take ye thought* for raiment?" (Matt. 6:28). Jesus made an important point with that comment. Thoughts are not forced upon you. They can be taken (accepted) or rejected. The choice is yours.

How is a thought "taken"? Jesus helped us out with this as well. He also said, "*Take no thought*, saying, What shall we eat . . ." (Matt. 6:31).

According to our Lord, you "take" a thought when you open

your mouth and speak out something based on that thought. Do not say something simply because it pops into your mind. When you say it, you take it. Do not take those thoughts of doubt and fear. Reject them by refusing to speak them out.

I am aware that it is easier to say this than to do it. Thoughts can be difficult to battle. But it is possible to battle thoughts and succeed. That is what I want to show you. You can neutralize a thought and render it harmless long before it has ever had a chance to germinate, take root, and grow.

Speak Out the Word of God

One of the most effective ways to silence a satanic suggestion or thought is to speak the opposite out loud, particularly when you can quote God's Word. Your mind cannot think one thing while your tongue is speaking something different. Try counting to ten in your mind, and in the middle of counting, say, "Hallelujah!" You will find that your counting stops when you begin to speak.

If you catch the devil trying to suggest a fearful thought in your mind, respond immediately by speaking Scriptures with your mouth.

You may say, "Pastor Dollar, can't I just think the Scripture verse? I don't want to embarrass myself."

No, you cannot just think a Bible verse and stop the wrong thought. I know you have already tried that, if you are like most of us, and found it does not work.

It only takes a millisecond to think a thought. You need to speak God's Word for a good long time to effectively neutralize an attack on your thought life. Also, when you speak the Word of God out loud, you reintroduce it to yourself through another of your sense gates—your ears. This gives you the added benefit of planting the powerful Word of God into your mind afresh and anew.

Speaking the Word is a powerful double-whammy to the devil. First, it stops the demonic thought dead in its tracks. Then it follows up by attacking that thought with the audible Word of God. As you will remember, ". . . faith cometh by hearing, and hearing by the word of God" (Rom. 10:17). Where faith is, fear cannot be.

Do not let fear of embarrassment keep you from speaking the Word out loud, even in public. So what if people think you are crazy? Remember what fear of people will do? Which is more important: your spiritual health and well-being or some stranger's opinion of you?

You need to open your mouth and say the right things. God designed you so that your heart and mouth work together.

For with the heart man believeth unto righteousness; and with the mouth confession is made unto salvation.

Romans 10:10

Rebuke Wrong Thoughts

God has given us spiritual weaponry with which to battle the thoughts and suggestions of the devil. One of the most powerful of these weapons is "rebuking." Just as with the previous suggestion, rebuking evil thoughts must be done with the spoken Word.

How do you rebuke a fearful thought? Actually, this is a simple thing to do. Just say, "In the name of Jesus, I will not have this thought in my mind! I have been delivered from fear!"

You may wonder how effective rebuking a thought can be. It is highly effective to the degree that you understand your authority as a believer and the power of the name of Jesus.

God's Word says:

> *That at the name of Jesus every knee should bow, of things in heaven, and things in earth, and things under the earth;*
> *And that every tongue should confess that Jesus Christ is Lord, to the glory of God the Father.*

> Philippians 2:10,11

Devils tremble at the mention of Jesus. This is doubly true when that exalted name is wielded by a believer who knows who he or she is in Jesus. Do not ever underestimate the power of a rebuke that comes from your lips. The very authority of Jesus Christ Himself has been vested in you as a child of the Most High God. You have been raised up with Jesus and seated with Him in heavenly places at the right hand of the Father. (Eph. 2:6.)

Do not just sit there and let the devil bombard your mind with thoughts of fear. Do not live with that torment. Rebuke him, and expect the devil to flee. If thoughts of failure begin to flood your mind, say:

"No, sir! I'm not going to be a failure. God didn't create me to fail. He has made me more than a conqueror. Therefore, I rebuke and renounce failure out of my thinking pattern right now. Failure, you are not part of my thoughts!"

Get aggressive and warlike when confronted with thoughts of fear.

Cut Thoughts Down

Thoughts are powerful things. Give them enough time and attention, and they will have you doing and saying things you would never dream of doing and saying.

"The devil made me do it" is a popular "cop out" when a Christian is caught in a sin. I have news for you! If you get caught up in sin, it is not because the devil made you do it. More than likely, it is because you let thoughts turn into imaginations, and imaginations led to actions.

No one gets "blindsided" by adultery. You do not get ambushed and find yourself in bed with someone else. If you succumb to adultery, it is because you invested time thinking about the possibility, imagining it, and fantasizing about it.

The devil will tell you, "A little fantasy won't hurt anything. It's not like you're really doing anything wrong." Do not fall for *this* thought. It is a lie.

Spend some time thinking about a sin, and I guarantee you that the devil will eventually present you with an opportunity to do it. Then, when you need the will to resist temptation, it is gone. You have no power to put down the act, because your thought life has been focused on sin. Thoughts invariably lead to actions.

Thoughts can change the very nature of who you are. For example, in spite of what the news media would have you believe, no one is born a homosexual. That kind of sexual lifestyle begins with a thought. Thoughts lead to imaginations. Imaginations lead to actions that ultimately change your nature, your mannerisms, perhaps even the very physiology of your brain.

The wonderful news is that those patterns can be broken. You break them by getting at the root. You received a thought, which was a seed. You did not deal with the seed, and it produced a harvest. Then your body lined up with that thought. If you want to get out of this kind of life, pull that seed up from the root and be what God has called you to be. I cannot over-emphasize how vital it is that you learn to deal with unholy thoughts.

One of the best methods for doing so is found in 2 Corinthians 10:5:

> *Casting down imaginations, and every high thing that exalteth itself against the knowledge of God, and bringing into captivity every thought to the obedience of Christ.*

What did Paul tell us to do in that verse? He said to cast down imaginations. What kind of imaginations was he talking about? We find out what kind of thoughts by reading the rest of that verse. We are to cast down those thoughts that do not line up with the will and Word of God. We are to measure every thought and every imagination that comes into our minds against the standard of God's Word and character. If a thought does not line up, cast it down!

As you can see, your imagination is a potent tool. God meant it to be that way. He gave us imaginations in order to enable us to "see" ourselves healed, prosperous, promoted, and blessed. Just as evil imaginations can turn you into an evil person, dwelling on holy thoughts and images can change you into the person God's Word says you should be.

In 2 Corinthians 10:5, Paul also told us to bring every thought captive to obedience. This represents another method of controlling your thought life. You have the ability to capture thoughts that run contrary to what you know Jesus wants you to do.

Another word for *capture* is "arrest." In a very real sense, this verse is telling you to arrest thoughts that trespass in your mind.

When a thought of doubt or fear gets planted in your mind, simply say, "Hold it right there! You are contrary to my obedience in Christ. You are under arrest."

This is a method of "policing" your thought life and keeping it free from seeds of fear.

Take the Next Step

Once you have arrested or cast down a fear-producing thought or imagination, it is important to take another step. When you remove something, you must replace it with something else. This is especially true when it comes to thoughts.

Have you ever tried to think about nothing? It is impossible. The human mind does not work that way. When you remove an evil thought, you must immediately replace it with something else. Otherwise, the enemy will slip right back in with another evil thought.

What kind of thought should you put in place of a thought you have just arrested? Philippians 4:8 has some good suggestions:

Finally, brethren, whatsoever things are true, whatso-
ever things are honest, whatsoever things are just,
whatsoever things are pure, whatsoever things are
lovely, whatsoever things are of good report; if there be
any virtue, and if there be any praise, think on these
things.

Your mind is like a computer. "Garbage in, garbage out" is what computer programmers say. Well, you can program your mind with things that are true, honest, just, pure, lovely, of good report, virtuous, and praiseworthy. The more you do, the more likely you will be to respond correctly when the pressure is on.

God has provided still another help for us in staying free of fear, and that is angels.

Declare War on Fear!

Finally, brethren, whatsoever things are true, whatsoever things honest, whatsoever things are just, whatsoever things are pure, whatsoever things are lovely, whatsoever things are of good report; if there by any virtue, and if there be any praise, think on these things.

Philippians 4:8

My prayer in the power of the Word . . .

_____

_____

_____

_____

_____

_____

_____

Study Questions

1. When do you find yourself struggling with thoughts of fear?

_____

_____

_____

_____

_____

2. How can we rebuke wrong thoughts?

_____

_____

_____

_____

3. What can we do to cut our thoughts down?

_____

_____

_____

_____

4. If you were going to replace your fearful thoughts with something else, what would you meditate on?

_____

_____

_____

_____

_____

10

Understanding Angel Power: A Death Blow to Fear

Do you believe in angels? Of course, if you are a Bible-believing Christian, your answer is yes. But how aware are you of their ministry? How many times a day do you think about the presence and work of angels?

If you are like most believers, your answer to the last two questions is, "Almost never."

That is sad, because the Bible has a great deal to say about the ministry of angels. Understanding and appropriating the power of angelic protection is one of the most effective ways to live free from the paralysis and bondage of fear.

You may be thinking, "What do you mean by 'appropriating the power of angelic protection'? I thought angels were just God's messengers."

That is a mistake a lot of believers make. Look with me at Hebrews 1:13,14, and you will begin to see what I mean.

*But to which of the angels said he at any time, Sit on
my right hand, until I make thine enemies thy foot-
stool?*

*Are they not all ministering spirits, sent forth to
minister for them who shall be heirs of salvation?*

In those verses God's Word tells us that angels are ministering spirits.

To whom did the author of Hebrews say angels minister?
He said they minister to those who are heirs of salvation. That
is you and me—and all those who are born again. We are heirs
according to the promise made to Abraham. (Rom. 8:17.)

What types of things do angels minister to us?

They minister all of the things that come with salvation.

The Greek word translated salvation in the New Testa-
ment is soteria, which means "safety, protection, health, healing, deliverance, and soundness." Today, angels function to
bring you the things that are part of your covenant of salvation. They are "covenant enforcers."

Where Have My Angels Been?

You may be wondering, "If I have all of these angels working
for me, why am I still getting beaten up by life?"

The answer is simple. The ministry of angels, just as everything else in the Christian life, is accessed by faith.

Healing is available to every believer; but, do all believers walk in healing? Obviously, they do not. The only believers who walk in divine health are those who recognize that health is one of their covenant benefits and who appropriate it by faith.

Financial security is promised to every Christian, yet only those who stand on God's promises of provision see any results.

The truth is that every spiritual benefit promised to the believer must be activated by faith to be manifested. This is true for angelic ministry as well. The reason so few are enjoying the service of God's mighty angels is that few of us have seen that promise clearly enough in the Word to have faith in it.

We are going to take a brief tour of the Scriptures in reference to angels. I believe when we are through, there will be no doubt in your mind that angels are present to help you.

Understanding angel power can deal a death blow to the spirit of fear in your life.

We Are Surrounded by Protection

In 2 Kings 6, we find a remarkable instance of angelic protection. The king of Syria was tired of the prophet Elisha knowing about his battle plans and telling the king of Israel beforehand. Apparently, Elisha knew from the Lord what the king was planning to do even before his generals did!

As a result, the king sent his meanest troops to find and kill Elisha. One morning, Elisha and his servant Gehazi woke up to find themselves surrounded by Syrian troops.

And when the servant of the man of God was risen
early, and gone forth, behold, an host compassed the
city both with horses and chariots. And his servant said
unto him, Alas, my master! how shall we do?

2 Kings 6:15

Understandably, Gehazi was disturbed. As best he could tell, he and his master were about to die. But Elisha was not bothered one bit. In fact, his response did not make sense to Gehazi at all.

And he answered, Fear not: for they that be with us
are more than they that be with them.

2 Kings 6:16

In other words, Elisha was saying, "Relax, Gehazi, we have them outnumbered."

At this point, the servant probably thought the prophet had lost his mind! It was obvious to him that there were only two of them and hundreds of the bad guys.

Why did one of these two men respond with fear and the other with calm assurance? The difference was that Elisha understood his covenant with God through Abraham.

Understanding the strength of God's covenant gives you

peace, even in the most desperate circumstances. Being covenant-minded gives you spiritual eyes.

> *And Elisha prayed, and said, LORD, I pray thee, open his eyes, that he may see. And the LORD opened the eyes of the young man; and he saw: and, behold, the mountain was full of horses and chariots of fire round about Elisha.*

> 2 Kings 6:17

Suddenly, Gehazi became aware of what Elisha had known all along: When you are in covenant with the Most High God, His angels surround you with protection 24 hours a day. Like Elisha, you are surrounded by protecting angels right now. And, just as with the prophet, they are waiting for your words of confidence and faith—words that are consistent with your blood covenant with God through Jesus—so they can go into action.

Child of God, you need to have your eyes opened. You need to realize that, no matter how many enemies the devil sends against you, there are more of you than there are of them. You have them outnumbered.

How do you put your angels to work? You do this by doing what Elisha did: Declare your covenant, and speak out the promises of God.

Some people may say, "If I could see some angels, then I would believe."

Jesus said, "Blessed are they that have not seen, and yet have believed." (John 20:29.)

If you want to see your angels, see them in your covenant with the eyes of faith. They are there because God says they are there. That ought to be enough for us.

The Promise Police

Now let us look at the activity of angels from a slightly different perspective as found in Galatians 3:19.

> *Wherefore then serveth the law? It was added because of transgressions, till the seed should come to whom the promise was made;* **and it was ordained by angels** *in the hand of a mediator.*

The aspect of this verse that I want you to see is that the law was *ordained by angels*. Another way of translating that is to say that the law "was put into effect" by angels.

So we see that one of the functions of angels is "to put into effect" the promises of the covenant. In other words, they are "covenant-enforcers."

Policemen sometimes say, "I don't make the laws; I just enforce them."

That is precisely the role of angels. They are "policemen" in the spirit realm who enforce the provision of your covenant with God. They do this *if*, and this is a big *if*, you loose them to do their jobs.

Angels enforce God's Word.

When you speak the words of God in the form of the promises in the Bible, they go into action to enforce them.

For example, God's Word says that we were healed almost 2,000 years ago by the stripes laid on Jesus. (1 Pet. 2:24.)

When you speak out loud the Scriptures concerning healing and your covenant right to healing, angels spring into action to do what is necessary in the spirit realm to bring healing to you. They are enforcing the terms of the covenant.

The Covenant of Promise

The covenant God has chosen to make with us is many-faceted. It contains promises of eternal life, healing, provision, and much more.

One of the most exciting and reassuring parts of the covenant that we have with God is His promise of protection. Of the many passages of Scripture that speak of this covenant protection, none is more powerful and more all-encompassing than Psalm 91.

From start to finish, Psalm 91 declares God's covering of protection and safety over the believer. Every Christian would do well to memorize this glorious proclamation. However, for right now let us focus in on the portion of the psalm that describes the role of angels in keeping the believer safe.

Take a look at Psalm 91:11,12:

For he shall give his angels charge over thee, to keep thee in all thy ways.

They shall bear thee up in their hands, lest thou dash thy foot against a stone.

If you still have any lingering doubts about God assigning angels to protect you from harm, these verses should dispel them. Your promise of protection from God does not get any plainer than Psalm 91. God has given His angels *charge* over us. That word means "assignment." God has assigned angels to keep us in all our ways. All means all, everything without exception.

When you slept in your bed last night, you were not alone. Angels stood watch over you.

When you ride in a car, when you walk down the street, when you fly in a jet, the angels of God are carrying out their assignments to keep you in all your ways. They have orders to even keep you from dashing your foot against a stone.

Angelic protection is a powerful thing. It is not a good idea to come against a believer who understands and appropriates his right to covenant-enforcing angels.

I have heard people say, "Where were my angels when I got robbed last week?"

Their angels were the same place their healing was when they got sick—right there in the covenant waiting to be appropriated by faith.

Angels Are No Longer Hindered

Whenever the subject of angels is discussed, someone always brings up the incident in Daniel where an angel was hindered by a demonic principality. People wonder if our angels can be held up in this manner.

Before we answer that, let us look at the passage of Scripture in question.

> In those days I Daniel was mourning three full weeks.
>
> I ate no pleasant bread, neither came flesh nor wine in my mouth, neither did I anoint myself at all, till three whole weeks were fulfilled.
>
> And in the four and twentieth day of the first month, as I was by the side of the great river, which is Hiddekel;
>
> Then I lifted up mine eyes, and looked, and behold a certain man clothed in linen, whose loins were girded with fine gold of Uphaz:
>
> His body also was like the beryl, and his face as the appearance of lightning, and his eyes as lamps of fire,

and his arms and his feet like in colour to polished
brass, and the voice of his words like the voice of a
multitude.

Daniel 10:2–6

After three weeks of fasting and waiting for an answer, Daniel finally experienced a breakthrough. Suddenly, he was visited by an angel. The appearance of this awesome and powerful "man" is a far cry from the images of chubby little children the world has envisioned as angels!

And he said unto me, O Daniel, a man greatly beloved,
understand the words that I speak unto thee, and stand
upright: for unto thee am I now sent. And when he had
spoken this word unto me, I stood trembling.

Daniel 10:11

After Daniel pulled himself together, the angel explained why it had taken three weeks for Daniel to receive his answer.

Then said he unto me, Fear not, Daniel: for from the
first day that thou didst set thine heart to understand,
and to chasten thyself before thy God, thy words were
heard, and I am come for thy words.

Daniel 10:12

Notice two things about the angel's words to Daniel:

Firstly, he told Daniel, in essence, "I have arrived in response to your words."

This confirms what we have seen elsewhere in the Bible: Angels listen to your words. When you speak covenant words of faith, angels leap into action.

Secondly, the angel told Daniel when he responded to Daniel's words, and that was the very first day he prayed. So why did it take three weeks for the angel to get to Daniel? The answer is in the very next verse.

> *But the prince of the kingdom of Persia withstood me one and twenty days: but, lo, Michael, one of the chief princes, came to help me; and I remained there with the kings of Persia.*

Daniel 10:13

This "prince of the kingdom of Persia" is a demonic principality. It resisted the angel, and they struggled for 21 days. Finally, the archangel Michael came in and helped the angel break through.

Can demonic powers hinder the angels of God like that now? No way! Satan was stripped of his authority in the spirit realm when Jesus defeated him, conquering death, hell, and the grave.

And having spoiled principalities and powers, he made a shew of them openly, triumphing over them in it.

Colossians 2:15

Who is gone into heaven, and is on the right hand of God; angels and authorities and powers being made subject unto him.

1 Peter 3:22

It is a whole new ball game since Jesus took his seat at the right hand of the Father. All authority in Heaven and on earth has been given to Jesus. As a result, the angels of God operate unhindered and unchallenged for those who speak God's words of promise.

Angels Listen to Our Words

If you want further evidence that the angels of God are listening to your words, look at Luke 12:8,9:

Also I say unto you, Whosoever shall confess me before men, him shall the Son of man also confess before the angels of God:
But he that denieth me before men shall be denied before the angels of God.

Your words are being heard by an audience of angels. How big is this audience? Revelation 5:11 tells us that the number of angels who surround the throne of God *is ten thousand times ten thousand, and thousands of thousands*. One scholar has calculated just this group of angels to amount to a trillion. That is ten thousand angels for every man, woman, and child alive on the earth today! And we do not know that the number mentioned is all of the angels in existence.

There is no shortage of angel power to put to work on your behalf. If as much as half of the earth's population became born again, there would still be 20,000 angels at each believer's disposal to carry out and enforce their covenant with God. Imagine 20,000 servants "on the mark, set, and ready to go" on your behalf!

As we have seen, a mighty host of angels is waiting to hear the Words of God come out of a believer's mouth. That fact is confirmed by Psalm 103:20:

> *Bless the LORD, ye his angels, that excel in strength,*
> *that do his commandments, hearkening unto the voice*
> *of his word.*

To *hearken* means "to listen for, to pay close attention to, and to hear and do." Angels are listening for the voice of God's Word. Give His Word voice, and they will respond.

When you have bills that need to be paid, speak the Word. Speak out things like this:

> *According to Philippians 4:19, my God shall supply all my needs according to His riches in glory by Christ Jesus. I am a tither, and according to Malachi 3:10, God is opening the windows of Heaven and pouring out a blessing for me that I will not have room to contain. Now, according to Hebrews 1:14, I command the angels of God to go forth and minister for me, an heir of salvation.*

When angels hear God's Word coming out of your mouth, they go into action, moving and influencing in the spirit realm to make God's covenant words come to pass for you.

What happens, on the other hand, when you speak out the same negative words of doubt and unbelief that the world speaks?

"Bills, bills, bills. We are never going to get caught up. They will probably turn off our lights before we see any money around here."

You have just taken your angels out of the picture. Those words run directly counter to what God's covenant says about your situation. In the presence of those words of doubt and unbelief, they have no choice but to bow their heads, fold their hands, and wait. They are waiting for you to speak God's Word and do it consistently enough for them to get some provision to you.

Your Wall of Safety

These principles are just as true when it comes to safety and security. Speaking what God's Word says about His protection of His children activates your angels to put up a wall around you that all of the forces in hell cannot break through. Look at Psalm 34:7:

> The angel of the LORD encampeth round about them
> that fear him, and delivereth them.

If you have battled fear, this is a great verse to speak about yourself on a daily basis.

You can speak out things like this: "Because I reverence the Lord, His angels camp around me and deliver me from all harm."

That is the kind of talk that will put angels in a position to do that very thing. No mugger, no rapist, no drive-by shooter on earth can penetrate that angelic shield of protection. And when you do find yourself in a sticky situation, this verse promises you deliverance.

This is the kind of angelic deliverance that the Apostle Peter experienced in Acts 12. He was in prison, scheduled for execution for preaching the Gospel. However, there were people praying for him, and he understood his covenant. So what happened?

> And, behold, the angel of the Lord came upon him, and a light shined in the prison: and he smote Peter on the side, and raised him up, saying, Arise up quickly. And his chains fell off from his hands.
> And the angel said unto him, Gird thyself, and bind on thy sandals. And so he did. And he saith unto him, Cast thy garment about thee, and follow me.
>
> Acts 12:7,8

How confident was Peter in his covenant of protection? He was scheduled to die in the morning, and yet the angel had to wake him up to break him out of prison! That is peace. That is confidence. That is the kind of freedom from fear that comes from knowing God's covenant of protection is being enforced by mighty angels.

Get Rid of That Fear

There is no place for fear in the life of a believer. The spirit of fear will rob you of everything that is sweet and good about the Christian life on this earth. It will steal your peace and torment your soul. But that is not the worst thing about fear.

The most devastating aspect of fear is that, as the reciprocal of faith, it opens the door to the very things you fear most, as we saw earlier in this book. It is time to get rid of fear! All of the steps you need to take to come out of fear and get into faith are actions:

- *Start changing* the way you talk.

- *Stop speaking* out words of fear and doubt.

- *Begin to speak* God's promises that apply to your situation.

- *Get a revelation* of the ministry of God's protecting angels.

- *See*—with your mind's eye—mighty warrior angels surrounding you on every side.

- *Do* these things, and the spirit of fear will be uprooted from your life. Then, look out! A lot of blessings, power, and peace are headed your way.

Declare War on Fear!

For he shall give his angels charge over thee, to keep thee in all thy ways.
They shall bear thee up in their hands, lest thou dash thy foot against a stone.

Psalm 91:11,12

My prayer in the power of the Word . . .

_____

_____

_____

_____

_____

_____

_____

Study Questions

1. How can we know we are surrounded by angels?

_____

_____

_____

_____

_____

2. What do angels do for us?

_____

_____

_____

_____

_____

3. What could you do in your own life to better team with the angels?

_____

_____

_____

_____

4. As you look back over this study, what have been the most important lessons you've learned?

_____

_____

_____

_____

_____

About the Author

Dr. Creflo A. Dollar is the founder and senior pastor of World Changers Church International (WCCI) in College Park, Georgia, and World Changers Church-New York. With 20 years of experience in ministry, Dr. Dollar is committed to bringing the Good News of Jesus Christ to people all over the world, literally changing the world one person at a time.

A former educational therapist, Dr. Dollar received the vision for World Changers in 1986. He held the church's first worship service in the cafeteria of Kathleen Mitchell Elementary School in College Park with only eight people in attendance. Over the years the ministry grew rapidly, and the congregation moved from the cafeteria to a modest-sized chapel, adding a weekly radio broadcast and four services each Sunday. On December 24, 1995, WCCI moved into its present location, the 8,500–seat sanctuary known as the World Dome. At a cost of nearly $20 million, the World Dome was built without any bank financing. The construction of the World Dome is a testament to the miracle-working power of

God and remains a model of debt-freedom that ministries all over the world emulate.

A native of College Park, Dr. Dollar received his bachelor's degree in educational therapy from West Georgia College and was awarded a Doctor of Divinity degree from Oral Roberts University in 1998. He is the publisher of *CHANGE*, an international quarterly lifestyle magazine with over 100,000 subscribers that gives Christians the tools they need to experience total life prosperity. His award-winning *Changing Your World* television broadcast reaches nearly one billion homes in practically every country in the world. A much sought-after conference speaker and author, Dr. Dollar is known for his practical approach to the Bible and has encouraged thousands to pursue a personal relationship with God. Dr. Dollar and his wife, Taffi, have five children and live in Atlanta.

Books by Dr. Creflo A. Dollar

In the Presence of God
Live Without Fear
Not Guilty
Love, Live, and Enjoy Life
Breaking Out of Trouble
Walking in the Confidence of God in Troubled Times